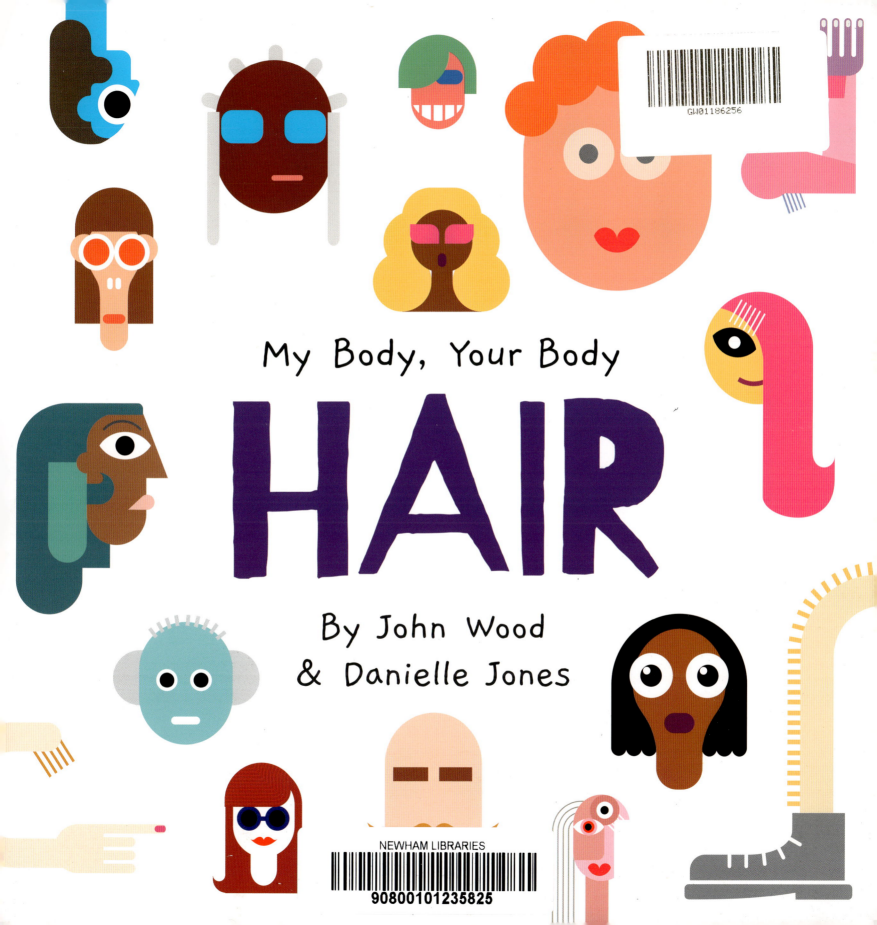

BookLife
PUBLISHING

©This edition published in 2023. First published in 2019.
BookLife Publishing Ltd.
King's Lynn, Norfolk, PE30 4LS, UK

All rights reserved. Printed in China.
A catalogue record for this book is available
from the British Library.

HB ISBN: 978-1-78637-742-5
PB ISBN: 978-1-80505-374-3

Written by: John Wood

Edited by: Madeline Tyler

Designed by: Danielle Jones

*All facts, statistics, web addresses and URLs
in this book were verified as valid and accurate at
time of writing. No responsibility for any changes to
external websites or references can be accepted by
either the author or publisher.*

All images are courtesy of danjazzia via
Shutterstock.com, unless otherwise specified.
With thanks to Getty Images, Thinkstock Photo
and iStockphoto. Additional illustrations by Danielle
Jones.

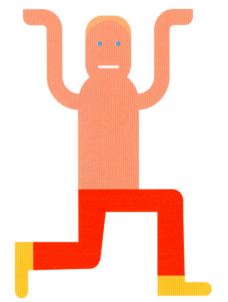

This is my hair.

And that is your hair.

Hair is EVERYWHERE.

3

Hair can be combed.

Hair can be straight.

Hair can be curly and frizzy and GREAT.

Hair can be thin and as

flat as the ground.

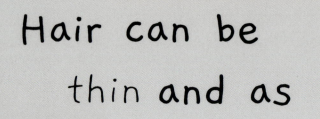

Hair can be THICK, and it will not stay down! 7

Hair can be orange, green, blue, black or brown.

Hair can be
yellow and
bright like
a crown.

Hair can be short.

Hair can be neat.

Hair can be long and fall down to your feet!

Hair can be tied in a tail or a **bunch**.

Some of us don't have much hair on our heads.

Some of us wear a BIG hat there instead.

15

Gran's hair is silver
and up in a bun.

Grandad is different.
Grandad has NONE!

This is the **muddiest** hair I have seen!

Go to the bathtub and get that hair **clean!**

Grown-ups grow hair on their arms and their legs.

In armpits, on backs — not just on the head.

This face is **bristly** and covered with hair.

This face is **smooth**.
It is totally bare.

We would go on.
Oh, if only we could!
All hair is **different** and **lovely**
and **good**.